Fun facts about birds: A multilingual pictionary in English, Azerbaijani, Kurdish, Turkish and Farsi
First published in 2026 by Englishazerbaijani
Copyright © 2026 Englishazerbaijani
All rights reserved. No portion of this book may be reproduced in any form without permission from the publisher, except as permitted by U.S. copyright law.
For permissions contact: Englishazerbaijani@gmail.com
ISBN: 978-1-7379401-5-9
Printed in the United States of America

PAPAQ* PHOTO BOOTH!

STICK YOUR PHOTO UNDER ONE OF THE AZERBAIJANI HATS BELOW TO BECOME AZERBAIJANI!

THIS BOOK BELONGS TO

....

* Traditional Azerbaijani hat.

DON'T FORGET TO SHARE YOUR PHOTOS WITH US!

 Englishazerbaijani

 Englishazerbaijani@gmail.com

Note: Abbreviations used in this book: AZ= Azerbaijani TR= Turkish

English: Chicken
Turkic (AZ): Toyuq
Turkic (TR): Tavuk

تۆرکجه: توْیوُق
کوردی: مریشک
فارسی: مُرغْ

Have you ever wondered why chicken eggs come in slightly different colors? It's all because of the special genes inside the hens that decide the color of their eggs.

English: Cockerel

Turkic (AZ): Beçə

Turkic (TR): Horuz

تۆرکجه: بئچه

کوردی: کەڵەشێر، کەڵەباب

فارسی: خُروس جَوان

A cockerel is a young rooster who isn't even one year old yet! He's just a little guy, learning how to walk proudly and show off his feathers.

English: Crane

Turkic (AZ): Durna

Turkic (TR): Turna

تۆرکجه: دوُرنا

کوردی: قورینگ

فارسی: دُرنا

Cranes are very tall flyers! They stretch out their long wings and glide high in the sky, moving so smoothly it looks like they're dancing in the air.

English: Crow

Turkic (AZ): Qarğa

Turkic (TR): Karga

تۆرکجه: قارغا

کوردی: قشقەڵە، قەڵەڕەش

فارسی: کلاغ

Crows are clever birds! They love shiny things and might just swoop down to steal something sparkly like a piece of jewelry.

English: Dove

Turkic (AZ): Qumru

Turkic (TR): Kumru

تۆرکجه: قومرو، گؤیرچین

کوردی: کۆتری سپی

فارسی: قمری

Unlike most birds who snuggle their heads under their wings at bedtime, doves like to sleep sitting up. They're like little sleepy sentinels.

English: Duck
Turkic (AZ): Ördək
Turkic (TR): Ördek

تۆرکجه: اؤردك
کوردی: مراوی، سۆنه
فارسی: اُردك

Female ducks are picky when it comes to choosing a mate! They like males who can dance well. It's like a fun duck dance-off for love.

English: Eagle
Turkic (AZ): Qartal
Turkic (TR): Kartal

تۆرکجه: قارتال
کوردی: هەڵۆ
فارسی: عُقاب

Eagles have super eyesight! It's about 5 times better than ours, and they can spot things from really far away, up to 3 kilometers.

English: Goose
Turkic (AZ): Qaz
Turkic (TR): Kaz

تۆرکجه: قاز
کوردی: قاز
فارسی: غاز

Geese and other migrating birds fly in a V-shape to save energy. It's like they're flying together in a big team, helping each other along the way.

English: Hawk

Turkic (AZ): Qırpığı, Laçın

Turkic (TR): Doğan

تۆرکجه: قیٛرغیٛ، لاچیٛن

کوردی: باشوو

فارسی: قِرقی

Some hawks are super speedy! They can dive through the air at an incredible 240 kilometers per hour.

English: Ostrich

Turkic (AZ): Dəvəquşu

Turkic (TR): Devequşu

تۆرکجه: دوه قوشو

کوردی: وشترمرخ

فارسی: شترمرغ

Ostriches are the fastest runners in the bird world! They zoom across the ground faster than any other bird you've ever seen.

English: Owl
Turkic (AZ): Bayquş
Turkic (TR): Baykuş

تۆرکجه: بایقوش
کوردی: کوند
فارسی: جغد

Owls have amazing night vision! They can see in the dark better than most animals, which makes them great nighttime hunters.

English: Parrot
Turkic (AZ): Tutuquşu
Turkic (TR): Papağan

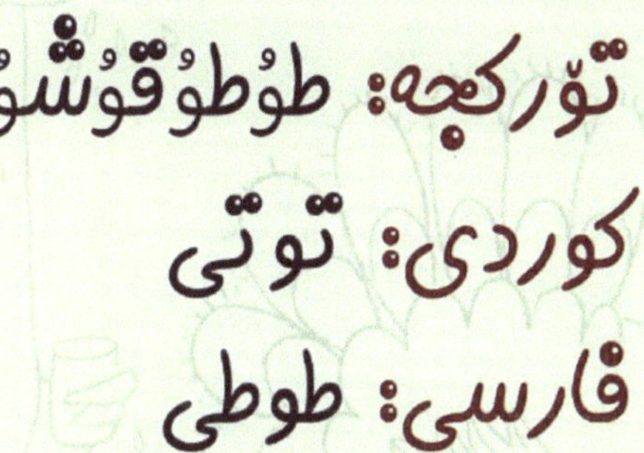

Parrots are special because they can mimic human speech! They're the only animals in the whole world that can do that.

English: Partridge
Turkic (AZ): Kəklik
Turkic (TR): Keklik

تۆرکجه: ککلیک
کوردی: کەو
فارسی: کَبك

Partridges lay the most eggs of any bird! Their nests are like egg factories, sometimes holding as many as 15 eggs at once.

English: Peacock

Turkic (AZ): Tovuzquşu

Turkic (TR): Tavuskuşu

تۆرکجه: طوْووزْ قوْشوْ

کوردی: تاوس

فارسی: طاووس

Those beautiful peacocks you see? They're actually all boys! They show off their bright and fancy feathers to impress the ladies.

English: Pinguin
Turkic (AZ): Pinqvin
Turkic (TR): Penguen

تۆرکجه: پینقوین
کوردی: پەنگوین
فارسی: پنگوئن

Gentoo penguins are super fast in the water! They swim faster than any other penguin, zooming along at up to 36 kilometers per hour.

English: Pigeon

Turkic (AZ): Göyərçin

Turkic (TR): Güvercin

تۆرکجه: گؤیرچین

کوردی: کۆتر

فارسی: کَبوتر

During the world wars, carrier pigeons were heroes! They delivered important messages that saved thousands of human lives.

English: Rooster
Turkic (AZ): Xoruz
Turkic (TR): Horuz

تۆرکجه: خوْروٗز
کوردی: کەڵەشێر، کەڵەباب
فارسی: خُروس

Roosters are like the protectors of the flock! They keep everything in order, find food for the hens, and even help them find cozy spots to lay their eggs.

English: Seagull
Turkic (AZ): Qağayı
Turkic (TR): Martı

تۆرکجه: قاغایی

کوردی: نەورەس

فارسی: مُرغ دَریایی

Seagulls can drink salty water! They have special glands above their eyes that help them get rid of all that salt so they can stay hydrated.

English: Sparrow

Turkic (AZ): Sərçə

Turkic (TR): Serçe

تۆرکجه: سئرچه

کوردی: چۆلەکە

فارسی: گُنجِشک

Sparrows are musical birds! In Canada, they're changing their tune from a three-note melody to a two-note one.

English: Stork
Turkic (AZ): Leylək
Turkic (TR): Leylek

تۆرکجه: لئیلك
کوردی: حاجی لەک لەک
فارسی: لک لک

Did you know that people used to believe storks delivered babies? It's a fun old tale.

English: Swan
Turkic (AZ): Qu
Turkic (TR): Kuğu

تۆرکجه: قوُ
کوردی: قوو
فارسی: قو

Swans are lovebirds! They often stay with the same mate for years and years, sometimes even their whole lives.

English: Turkey
Turkic (AZ): Hinduşka
Turkic (TR): Hindi

تۆرکجه: هیندوشکا، هشترخان
کوردی: قەل
فارسی: بوقلمون

You can tell the gender of a turkey by its droppings! Males make spiral-shaped poop, while females make poop shaped like the letter J.

English: Vulture

Turkic (AZ): Leşyeyən, Akbaba

Turkic (TR): Akbaba

تۆرکجه: لئش یئین، آکبابا

کوردی: داڵ

فارسی: کَرکَس

Some vultures have a gross but effective defense mechanism! When threatened, they vomit up strong stomach acids to scare away predators and make a quick escape.

English: Woodpecker
Turkic (AZ): Ağac dələn
Turkic (TR): Ağaçkakan

تۆرکجه: آغاج دلن
کوردی: دارکونکەر
فارسی: دارکوب

Woodpeckers have a preference for dead trees! They peck away at them to find bugs to eat and make cozy homes.

ABOUT ENGLISHAZERBAIJANI

Azerbaijani is a Turkic language spoken mainly in Iran and the Republic of Azerbaijan. EnglishAzerbaijani is a creative platform that produces books, videos, animations, and educational materials in both Azerbaijani and English, celebrating culture and diversity.

Our content helps children connect with their heritage while building language skills, expanding vocabulary, and discovering other cultures. Through engaging visuals and interactive storytelling, EnglishAzerbaijani makes learning Azerbaijani language and culture fun and accessible for kids and learners of all ages.

You are WONDERFUL!

Please do not forget to review us on amazon. Your reviews matter and help us improve!

Tag us on social media because we LOVE hearing from you!

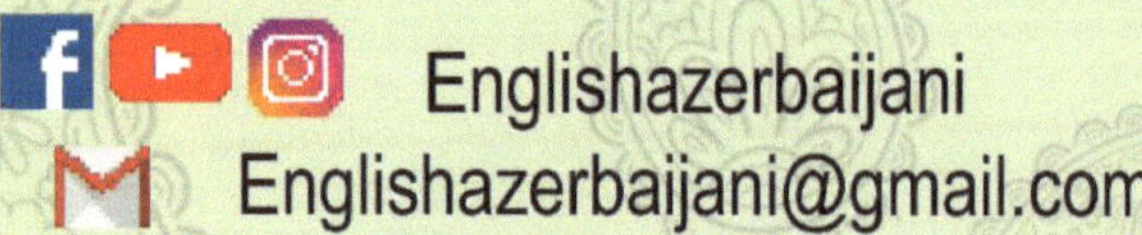

Englishazerbaijani

Englishazerbaijani@gmail.com

HOLD YOUR ROOTS TIGHT!

MORE BOOKS BY THE SAME AUTHOR!

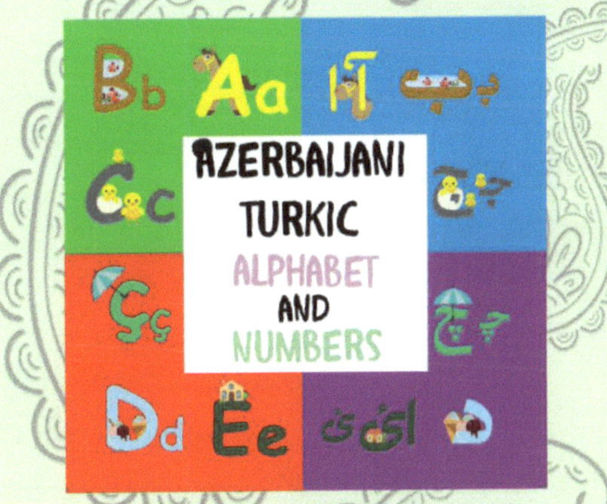

Are you looking for a simple and easy way to learn Azerbaijani alphabet and numbers? Try out our book!

BOOKS CAN BE FOUND ON AMAZON!

"Which animal is more useful?" is created to deliver the important message of acceptance, confidence and understanding of happiness using attractive child-friendly illustrations and comprehensible examples in English and Azerbaijani Turkic. In addition to helping with language development, this book will give children a fuller understanding of themselves and others, and teaches them to learn and embrace that everyone is different and that's a beautiful part of our life.

BEST-SELLER BOOK, JIRTDAN'S HALLOWEEN!

Jirtdan is a figure from Azerbaijani folklore, a tale familiar to all Azerbaijani people, passed down through generations. Jirtdan is a tiny kid who, despite his size, uses his superior brain to discover innovative solutions to his problems. Originally, in the tale passed through oral storytelling, Jirtdan and his companions venture into the forests to gather firewood and become lost. They are captured by an ogre until Jirtdan tricks the beast and frees them, occupying the ogre until all the children are safely away.

In this twist on the timeless tale, Jirtdan and his friends journey together on a grand adventure to Disney World.

Similar to the original story, Jirtdan uses his wits to persuade others into doing his chores.

The old and new tales intertwine again when a monstrous ogre captures the kids and holds them hostage. The trickster Jirtdan must exercise his wits to save himself and his friends before it is too late.

The kids in this story bob for Guba apples, see all the fantastic things they've never experienced and have a wonderful time in this fascinating new world. With a Halloween twist and just the right amount of spookiness for little readers, this retelling packed with cultural lessons and old traditions is sure to delight and educate readers of all ages.

MORE BOOKS BY THE SAME AUTHOR!
FUN FACTS ABOUT ANIMALS
A Multilingual Pictionary In English, Azerbaijani, Turkish Kurdish and Farsi
By: Darya Hodaei
Illustrator: Maedeh Ramharand
FUN FACTS ABOUT FRUITS
A Multilingual Pictionary In English, Azerbaijani, Turkish, Kurdish and Farsi
By: Darya Hodaei
Illustrator: Maedeh Ramharand
TRY FUN FACTS ABOUT ANIMALS AND FRUITS TOO!

KOROGHLU THE HERO!

Koroghlu—whose name means "Son of the Blind"—is a legendary hero celebrated across Turkic cultures. Koroghlu the Hero tells the story of his life, bringing to life his courage, cleverness, and steadfast commitment to justice as he stood up for ordinary people against oppression. The legend of Koroghlu has been cherished for generations in places like Iran, Azerbaijan, Turkey, Turkmenistan, and Central Asia and remains an important part of cultural heritage. Explore the life of Koroghlu in this captivating story by Darya Hodaei, brought to life with vibrant, colorful illustrations by Mahsa Hasanpur.

PRONUNCIATION REFRENCE TABLE

Azerbaijani letters in Iran	Azerbaijani Letters in the republic of Azerbaijan	IPA symbol (Pronounciation)	Example in English	Example in Azerbaijani	
آ، ا	A, a	ɑ	Hot /hɑt/	Nar /nɑr/	نار
ب	B, b	b	Book /bʊk/	Baba /bɑbɑ/	بابا
ج	C, c	dʒ	Judge /dʒʌdʒ/	Can /dʒɑn/	جان
چ	Ç, ç	tʃ	Church /tʃə:tʃ/	Aç /ɑtʃ/	آچ
د	D, d	d	Door /dɔɹ/	Ad /ɑd/	آد
ائ، ئ	E, e	e	Dress /dres/	Ev /ev/	ائو
آ، ه	Ə, ə	æ	Fat /fæt/	Əl /æl/	آل
ف	F, f	f	Fun /fʌn/	Kifir /ki:fi:r/	کیفیر
گ	G, g	ɟ	No EN word	Gəlin /ɟæli:n/	گلین
غ	Ğ, ğ	ɣ	No EN word	Oğlan /oɣlɑn/	اوْغلان
ح، ه	H, h	h	Hot /hɑt/	Hara /hɑrɑ/	هارا
خ	X, x	x	Loch /lɔx/	Ox /ox/	اوْخ
ایْ، یْ	I, ı	ɯ	Hook /hɯk/	Altı /ɑltɯ/	آلتیْ
ای، ی	İ, i	i:	Sheep /ʃi:p/	Bir /bi:r/	بیر
ژ	J, j	ʒ	Vision /ˈvɪʒ(ə)n/	Jurnal /ʒurnɑl/	ژورنال
ك	K, k	k	Cute /kju:t/	Kirpi /ki:rpi:/	کیرپی
ل	L, l	l	Lamp /læmp/	Lamp /lɑmp/	لامپ
م	M, m	m	Monkey /ˈmʌŋki/	Mən /mæn/	من
ن	N, n	n	Onion /ˈʌnjən/	Sən /sæn/	سن
اوْ، وْ	O, o	o	Hope /hoʊp/	Oğlan /oɣlɑn/	اوْغلان
اؤ، ؤ	Ö, ö	ø	No EN word	Öl /øl/	اؤل
پ	P, p	p	Pool /pu:l/	Öp /øp/	اؤپ
ق	Q, q	g	Good /gʊd/	Qal /gɑl/	قال
ر	R, r	r	Rose /rəʊz/	Əllər /ællær/	آللر
س	S, s	s	See /si:/	Sarı /sɑrɯ/	ساریْ
ش	Ş, ş	ʃ	Show /ʃo:/	Daş /dɑʃ/	داش
ت	T, t	t	Tea /ti:/	At /ɑt/	آت
اوُ، وُ	U, u	u	Boot /bu:t/	Uşaq /uʃɑg/	اوُشاق
اۆ، ۆ	Ü, ü	y:	Few /fjy:/	Gördüm/ɟørdy:m/	گؤردۆم
و	V, v	v	Violet /ˈvaɪələt/	Ver /ver/	وئر
ی	Y, y	j	Yellow /ˈjɛl.oʊ/	Yol /jol/	یوْل
ز	Z, z	z	Zoo /zu:/	Yüz /jy:z/	یۆز